A little practice and a few tests will help you achieve the color you want. The dye recipes in the pie charts on each swatch represent the color and quantity of dye needed to make that color. For darker shades use more dye, for paler shades use less dye with more water.

ALL ABOUT DYE

Welcome to the Technicolor world of dye! Dye has been used for thousands of years to color textiles, clothing, threads, yarns, wood, and even stone. There are many different kinds of dye. Natural dyes are made from leaves, minerals, vegetables, bark, berries, and flowers. Synthetic dyes are the most common and are made from chemicals. Be certain to pick the right kind of dye for the fabric content. Cotton and linen will accept any kind of dye, while wool needs aniline dyes. Working with dyes can be very messy and damaging if not handled carefully. Dye can be irritating or toxic on skin, so wear rubber gloves and old clothes you wouldn't mind getting dye on. Always work on a taped-down plastic drop cloth to save your floors. It is important to "set" the dye to make it permanent by following the instructions on the dye package. You may then wash your dyed fabrics in cold water to help maintain the color. Keep experimenting with techniques and colors and in no time you will be a dye expert!

TODD OLDHAM

Designed, written and photographed by Todd Oldham Studio:
Yoshi Funatani, Greg Kozatek, Tony Longoria, Hillary Moore & Jennifer Whitney
Models: Azra, Miranda, Saevar & Samir
Library of Congress: 2012930845 ISBN: 9781934429907

AMMO
AMERICAN MODERN BOOKS

candy-colored stripes
are a snap with this easy
dye technique

SNOW
CONE
DIP
DYE

SUPPLIES

YOU WILL NEED

two 10 inch aluminum pans, fabric dye, washed tank top, plastic drop cloth or garbage bags

1

Tape down a plastic drop cloth. Mix dyes well and pour 2 inches of dye into the pans. Wet the tank top and wring it out so it is just damp.

2

Place the dye pans next to each other and submerge the bottom 12 inches of the wet tank in the first pan. Let the next 8 inches submerge into the second pan and let set for 4-6 minutes.

3

Pull the tank top out of the dye, holding it from the top to avoid spilling dye on the un-dyed areas. Remove the first dye pan and place the bottom 6 inches of the tank into the second dye pan and let set for 6 minutes. Carefully remove and rinse the tank. "Set" the dye following the instructions on the dye container.

FOLD UP

UP

origami and painting add a
new fold to pinstriped shirts

BUTTON DOWN

SUPPLIES

1 Put down a drop cloth and mix fabric dye in a glass jar. Iron the first crease in your shirt by folding the right sleeve over towards the left and iron flat as shown.

2 Pleat and iron 1 ½ inch folds towards the button placket.

3 Repeat on the other side until the entire folded bottom of the shirt stacks flat as shown. Re-press them all flat and line the pleat edges up. Secure folds with a rubber band.

4 Iron the sleeves flat. Pleat and iron in 1 ½ inch folds from the cuff up to the shoulder. Secure the folds with a rubber band.

5 Remove the rubber band from the bottom pleats and place on drop cloth. Use a sponge brush to apply dye to the outside folded edges of the pleats, stopping at the armhole. Apply dye in light strokes. The sponge brush should not be dripping while you paint.

6 Open the bottom up and lay out on the drop cloth. Repeat the painting technique on the sleeves.

7 Rinse and "set" the shirt as directed on the fabric dye container. Iron the shirt flat to best show the beautiful new stripes!

FAN
FOLD
FRENZY

origami and dye join
forces to create
one-of-a-kind pinstripes

YOU WILL NEED
four colors of fabric dye, four glass jars
to mix dye in, drop cloth, iron, sponge,
brushes, washed t-shirt

SUPPLIES

1 Iron flat 2 ½ inch folds diagonally from
the lower left corner of the t-shirt towards
the right sleeve as shown.

Iron each pleat as you go.

2

3 Continue pleating while making sure
the folds line up on both sides.

4 Align all folded edges and re-press edges flat.

On a drop cloth mix two colors of dye in two jars. Place the pleated t-shirt on the drop cloth. Paint one color of dye on the edge of one side of the folds with a non-dripping sponge brush.

5

6 Paint the opposite side of the pleated fold with the second dye color.

Rinse and set the dye according to the instructions on the dye container. Dry and iron flat.

7

8 Repeat the pleating process starting at the lower right corner towards the left sleeve and ironing each edge.

Align the fold edges and re-press them flat

9

10 Mix up the remaining two dye colors in glass jars. Paint along on the side of the fold with one of the dyes.

Paint the other side of folds with the last dye color and rinse out. "Set" according to the instructions on the dye box and enjoy!

11

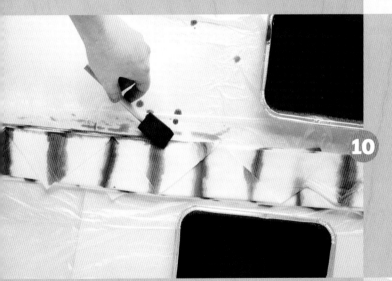

paint with dry dye
straight from the box

DRY
DYE
DIFFUSION

YOU WILL NEED
dry dye, tank top, drop cloth

Wet the tank top and lightly wring it out until it is not dripping. Clip off a small corner of the powdered dye packet and sprinkle it on the tank in a stripe.

1

2

Continue sprinkling on another dye color.

When your design is complete, watch it closely to determine when you want to rinse it out and stop the dye from dissolving. The longer the dye sits on the tank the more diffused it will become. Rinse and "set" the dye following the directions on the box.

3

MIX
EFFECT
REMIX

combine several classic
tie-dye techniques
for brand new effects

YOU WILL NEED
dye, 12 x 8 inch aluminum roasting pans, iron, sponge brush, rubber bands, washed t-shirt

1

Dip dye the top of the t-shirt using the directions on page 7.

Pinch the fabric in the center of the chest to create the sunburst.

2

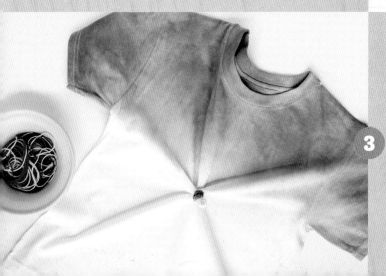

3

Secure a rubber band onto the pinch so about 1 inch of fabric is sticking out of the rubber band.

Add two more rubber bands 1 inch apart.

4

5 Repeat adding rubber bands on the back center.

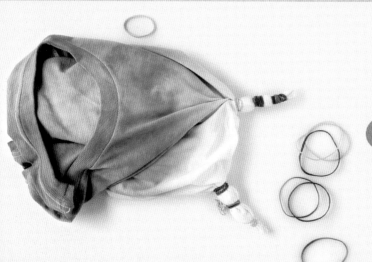

Repeat the same three rubber bands, starting under one of the armholes.

6

7 Mix another color of dye and fill a pan 2 ½ inches. Submerge the rubber-banded points in the dye for 6 minutes.

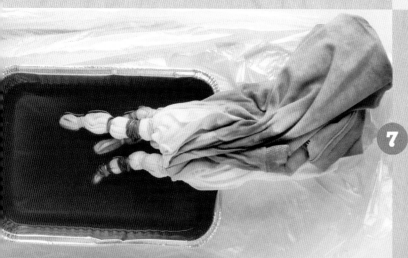

Rinse and remove rubber bands.
Let t-shirt dry and iron flat.

8

9

Fold the hem up and make 2 inch
pleats up towards the sleeves.

Align the folds and re-press them flat.

10

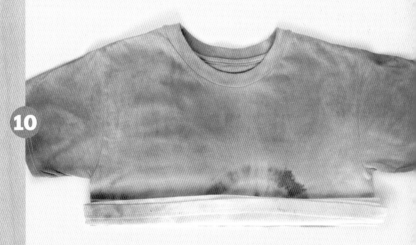

11

Mix another color of dye and paint up
both sides of the folds with a sponge
brush to create the waves in the ocean
sunset pattern. Rinse and "set" the dye
as per the instructions on the dye box.

create a galaxy of color
using frozen dye cubes

FREEZE
STYLE

YOU WILL NEED
dye, ice cube trays, plastic sandwich bags, hammer, cloth for hammering, washed t-shirt

1

Prepare dye colors and freeze them in ice cube trays. Place the frozen cubes in plastic bags.

2

Place the cloth on top of the bag and lightly break the cubes apart with the hammer.

3

This part can get messy so best to do this outside. Sprinkle the frozen dye onto the t-shirt as you like.

4

Continue sprinkling the frozen dye until your design is complete.

5

Watch the dye diffuse and blend and then shake the dye off when you feel the design in finished. Rinse and "set" per the box instructions.

ICE SHEETS

frozen dye cubes are all you need to create this cool dotted sheet

YOU WILL NEED

dye, ice cube trays, washed bed sheet

1. Prepare and freeze the dye colors in ice trays.

2. Carefully place the frozen cubes directly on the sheet.

3. Complete your pattern, allowing space between the cubes for the dye to spread out while melting.

4. Shake the cubes off when you are happy with the design and rinse. "Set" the dye following the dye box instructions.

SUPPLIES

1

2

3

4

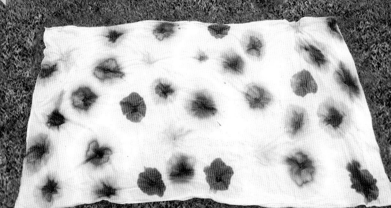

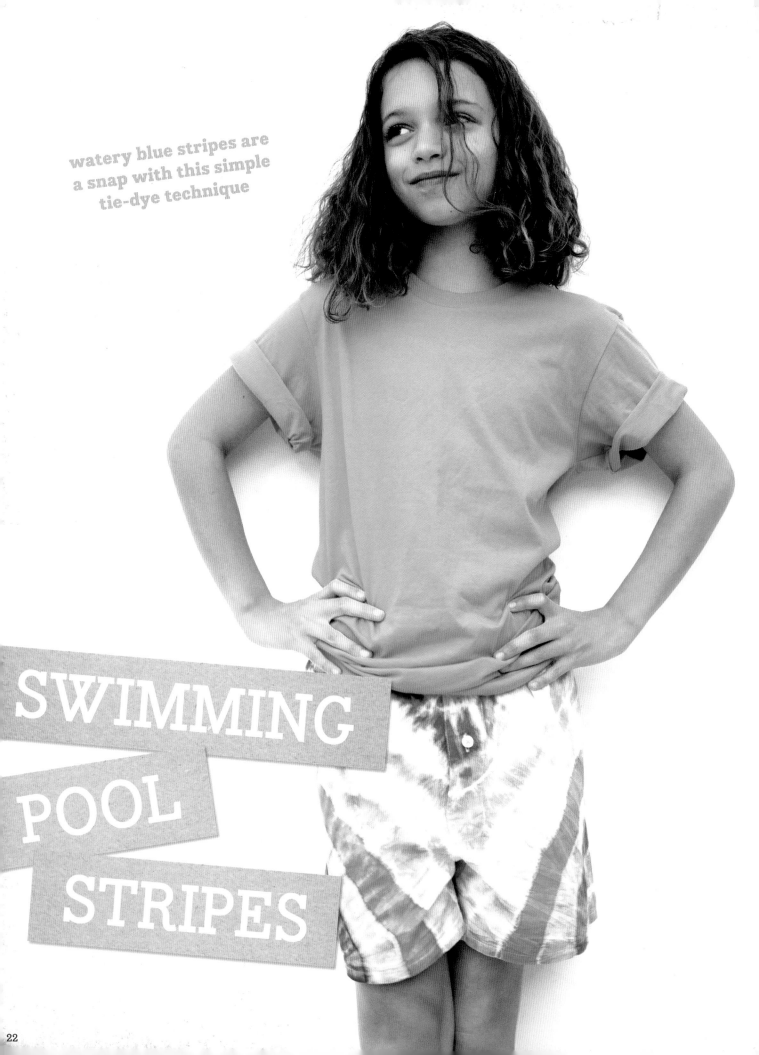

watery blue stripes are
a snap with this simple
tie-dye technique

SWIMMING POOL STRIPES

YOU WILL NEED
dye, rubber bands, 10 inch x 8 inch aluminum pans, sponge brushes, drop cloth, washed boxer shorts

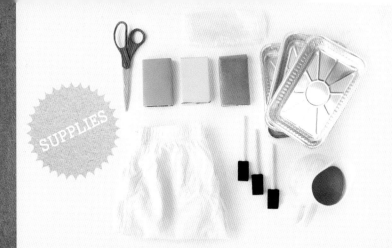

SUPPLIES

1 Starting at the hem, secure rubber bands about 1 inch apart as shown.

2 Continue securing rubber bands until you reach the center seam of the boxers. Repeat on the other side as shown.

3 Divide the remaining fabric at the waistband into two sections and secure the rubber bands as before.

4 Repeat this on the other side until you have 6 rubber-banded sections.

Mix the dye colors well. **5**

6 Lay down a drop cloth and pour the dye into the aluminum pans.

7 Use a sponge brush to paint alternating colors on the un-banded areas and let set for 8 minutes.

Submerge the boxers into a medium-toned dye color and let set for 6 minutes.

8

9 Remove rubber bands and rinse well. "Set" the dye by following the instructions on the dye box.

create super simple
psychedelia in seconds

OLD
SCHOOL
WRAP

YOU WILL NEED
aluminum pan, string, washed t-shirt, drop cloth, scissors

1 Make a pinch in the center front of the chest area.

2 Tie a knot around the pinch with the string and start tightly winding up the t-shirt as shown.

3 Continue tightly wrapping across the shirt until you reach the center back area and tie the string off with a knot.

4 On a drop cloth, mix dye and pour 3 inches into the pan. Submerge the tied-up t-shirt and let soak for 10 minutes.

5 Remove, rinse, and carefully cut the string.

6 Unwind the string from the t-shirt.

7 Re-rinse the t-shirt and "set" the dye by following the instructions on the dye box.

bricks of bold color
brighten up any tote

TECHNICOLOR

DREAM

TOTE